baseball

the
SUMMER OLYMPICS

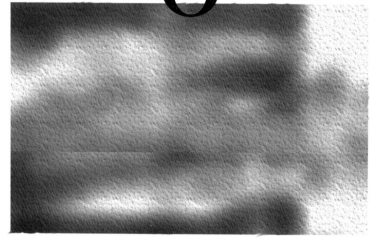

baseball

PUBLISHED BY SMART APPLE MEDIA

Published by Smart Apple Media
123 South Broad Street, Mankato, Minnesota 56001

Cover Illustration by Eric Melhorn

Designed by Core Design

Photos by: Allsport, Bettmann Archives, Sports
Illustrated, Long Photography, Wide World Photos,
Freelance Photographers Group, Library of Congress

Library of Congress Cataloging-in-Publication Data

Plunkett, Bill, 1961-
Baseball / by Bill Plunkett.
(The Summer Olympics)
Includes index.
Summary: Traces the history of baseball as an Olympic
sport.

ISBN 1-887068-05-8

1. Baseball—Juvenile literature. 2. Olympics—Juvenile
literature. [1. Baseball—History. 2. Olympics.] I. Title.
II. Series.

GV867.5.P58 1995   95-11966
796.357—dc20

ABCDE

BASEBALL GOES INTERNATIONAL

Baseball has been played professionally in the United States for over 125 years. Considered the most American of all games, baseball combines teamwork with individual talent and asks players to display a number of skills as they run, throw, catch and hit. Such players as Babe Ruth, Mickey Mantle and Hank

Celebrating in Seoul in 1988.

All eyes are on the play at home plate.

Aaron became national heroes in the United States. Fans followed their favorite teams and favorite players, arguing over who was better, from Joe DiMaggio vs. Ted Williams to Barry Bonds vs. Ken Griffey, Jr.

But it wasn't until the second half of this century that baseball started to become popular elsewhere around the world, especially in Asia and South America. Baseball has grown so popular that it was finally added to the Olympics as a demonstration sport in 1984. Games were played and winners selected, but official medals were not given out or counted in a country's medal total.

Finally, in 1992, baseball was given official medal status. Showing just how much baseball has grown in other countries, the United States only managed a fourth-place finish, behind Cuba, Taiwan and Japan.

Baseball will once again be a hotly contested medal sport at the 1996 Summer Olympics in Atlanta. Will the Cubans continue to dominate the sport and defend their 1992 gold medal? Will a young U.S. team capture a medal in the game invented here? Or will there be an upset by some little-known team? Baseball fans from around the world are eagerly awaiting the answers to those questions.

Close plays keep the action suspenseful (pages 10-11).

PRE-1984: NOT READY YET

Prior to the 1984 games, baseball was occasionally played as an exhibition sport at the Olympics. These exhibitions were limited to two or three teams playing one or two games just for show, with no medals at stake.

The first exhibition game was played at the Summer Olympics in St. Louis in 1904, just 35 years after Henry Chadwick

The players look to the umpire for the call.

had published baseball's first official rulebook. Eight years later, another exhibition was played in Stockholm, Sweden. The United States assembled a baseball team with athletes from its track and field team. They played one game against a team of Swedish athletes and won 13-3.

At the Summer Games in 1936, over 100,000 fans were on hand in Berlin for Olympic competition when they got a novel bonus—a baseball game between an American team and a team of amateur players from various countries. The Americans lost.

Twenty years later, at the 1956 Olympic Games in Melbourne, Australia, a team of American servicemen beat an Australian team 11-5 in front of approximately 114,000 fans. It is believed to be the most fans to watch a baseball game in person.

One of the first official Olympic teams played in 1936.

In 1964, the Americans and two Japanese teams staged a two-game mini-tournament as part of the Olympics in Tokyo. The U.S. team won both games.

LOS ANGELES 1984: DEMO MODEL

Baseball was a natural at the 1984 Summer Olympics in Los Angeles, the first Games to be held in the United States since 1932. This time it was played as a demonstration sport. Demon-

World-class talent displays smart base-running.

stration sports are played at each Olympics as a test run for sports being considered for official Olympic status. For the first time, baseball players marched in the opening and closing ceremonies and stayed in the Olympic Village with the other athletes.

Eight teams played a tournament at Dodger Stadium, home of the Los Angeles Dodgers. The U.S. team included many players who went on to play major league baseball, including Will Clark, Barry Larkin, Mark McGwire, Cory Snyder and Shane Mack. As expected, the United States dominated the preliminary round, beating teams from Italy and the Dominican Republic 12-0 and 16-1, respectively.

The United States and Japan met in the championship game. During a warmup tour before the Olympics, the United States had beaten Japan six of seven times they played. But not this time. Japan beat Team USA 6-3 to win the gold medal. "It was the greatest victory in the history of Japanese baseball," said Japanese manager Reichi Matsunaga.

In the bronze-medal game, Chinese Taipei played Korea in a close contest. The game was scoreless until the 14th inning, when Chinese Taipei finally scored and won the game 3-0.

SEOUL 1988: FINAL WARMUP

Baseball was a demonstration sport again at Seoul, South Korea, in 1988. This time the United States was better at demonstrating its ability at the sport.

Again, the U.S. team had several players who would go on to play in the major leagues, including Robin Ventura, Tino Martinez and Bret Barberie. But the key players were a couple of future major-league pitchers—Ben McDonald and Jim Abbott.

McDonald had two complete-game victories for the United States in the preliminary rounds. He struck out seven players in a 7-2 victory over Puerto Rico that moved the United States into the gold-medal game against Japan.

He's out!

Abbott started the game against Japan. The American pitcher was one of the most popular players of the Olympics because of his inspirational story. Born without a right hand, Abbott overcame his disability and starred in high school, college and now the Olympics.

In the gold-medal game, Abbott gave up seven hits and struck out four while getting the Japanese batters to ground out 15 times. Martinez's three hits—including two home runs—drove in four runs to put the Americans on top 5-3.

"This is my number one thrill in sports," Abbott said. The next game he pitched was for the California Angels in 1989. He went straight from amateur baseball to the major leagues.

Puerto Rico beat South Korea, 7-0, to win the bronze medal.

BARCELONA 1992: FULL MEDAL STATUS

Eighty-eight years after the first baseball exhibition was played in the Olympics, the sport was given full medal status. Things had changed so much in that time that the Americans weren't even favored to win the gold medal. That distinction went to the national team from Cuba, a small island just off the coast of Florida. The Cuban team was called "The Other Dream Team" because they were expected to dominate the competition in Barcelona nearly as much as the American basketball "Dream Team" led by Magic Johnson, Michael Jordan and Larry Bird.

Cuban players were not allowed by their government to play professionally in the major leagues. Instead, they stayed together and formed the most talented amateur team in the world. Cuba boycotted the 1984 and 1988 Olympics, missing out on baseball's demonstration sport tournaments. But prior to 1992, Cuba had won 19 world championships and nine Pan American Games championships. In fact, from 1988 to 1992, the Cuban team lost only one game in international competition.

To the Cubans, baseball is more than a game, it is a way of life.

The Cubans were older than the American players. They had five players over age 30 and many others in their late 20s, while the Americans were all 18 to 22. The Americans had only played together for five weeks before the Olympics started and had lost five of seven exhibition games against the Cubans.

"Our system is different," American coach Ron Fraser explained. "We get a new international team each year."

The 1992 U.S. team included Jeffrey Hammonds, Charles Johnson, Phil Nevin, Darren Dreifort and Michael Tucker, who were all first-round draft picks by major-league teams. Cuba's stars were third baseman Omar Linares, shortstop German Mesa, second baseman Antonio Pacheco, outfielders Victor Mesa and Orestes Kindelan and pitchers Osvaldo Fernandez and Omar Ajete.

The level of skill in international play continues to improve.

A tough Cuban team dominated in 1992.

The Cubans breezed through the preliminary rounds, winning all seven games by a total score of 78-14. The Americans took heart in the fact that they lost by only three points, 9-6, which was closer than any other team Cuba played.

"We want one more shot at the Cubans," Nevin said. "If we played them 10 times, they might beat us seven. But, that gold-medal game is just one game. And, they can be beat."

The U.S. never made it to the gold-medal game, however. It lost to Japan 7-1 in the final game of the preliminary round. That loss meant the Americans had to play Cuba first in the medal round. The Cubans won 6-1 behind the pitching of Fernandez and Ajete. Japan lost to Taiwan in the other semifinal game, setting up a rematch with the United States. Japan won this one, too, 8-3, and got the bronze medal.

Taiwan played Cuba in the gold-medal game, losing 11-1. Cuba had 18 hits in the game, including home runs by Kindelan, Alberto Hernandez and Lazargo Vargas, who hit for the cycle (a single, double, triple and home run). Taiwan was held to just four hits.

The Cubans outscored their opponents 95-16 in winning all nine of their Olympic games on the way to baseball's first gold medal.

"To them, this is the World Series," said Ron Polk, an American college coach and former Team USA coach.

Home run! (pages 26-27)

"Baseball is our national sport," Cuban coach Jorge Fuentes said. "You come to Cuba and all you see is little boys trying to play baseball. It's a way of life. This is a highlight for Cuba."

IN THE OLYMPICS TO STAY

Recently, Olympic officials have allowed professionals to compete for medals in basketball, tennis and figure skating. In June 1994, the International Baseball Association considered opening the Olympics to professionals, too. However, it's very unlikely that major-league players will ever compete in the Olympics, because they would have to leave their professional teams in the middle of the season.

"Our best players are in the majors or the minors," said Fraser, who retired after the 1992 Olympics. "I don't think there'll ever be a Dream Team [of major leaguers] in baseball."

Not that Fraser minds. He feels that taking part in the Olympics is a valuable experience for young amateur players. What is most important—for fans and players alike—is that the game of baseball is finally being celebrated and contested in Olympic competition.

That competition should be more thrilling than ever in Atlanta in 1996. Baseball will be played from July 20 through August 4 at the new Atlanta Stadium, future home of the Atlanta

Braves. The outstanding Cuban team will have to overcome its country's economic problems, the aging of its star players and the defection of some young players to American professional leagues. Meanwhile, amateur programs in Asia are stronger than ever, as shown by their dominance in Little League World Series competitions. And the United States, the birthplace of baseball, continues to produce some of the best baseball players in the world.

A relative newcomer to the Olympic stage, baseball should provide sports fans with plenty of exciting moments at the 1996 Games in Atlanta.

Who will celebrate in Atlanta in 1996?

baseball

Inaugural Results—Final Standings 1992 Olympic Competition

Rank	Nation	Overall Record
1	Cuba	9-0
2	Chinese Taipei	6-3
3	Japan	6-3
4	USA	5-4
5	Puerto Rico	2-5
6	Dominican Republic	2-5
7	Italy	1-6
8	Spain	1-6